Skewered!

Oh, yuck. Just yuck . . . The probler
everything you put in yo
mouth . . . Who really wants to eat grape-
mustard sorbet? . . . Food is to eat, r
o fra
would   Frer
for 'fc   eg
i do   cu
and a   om
a lot . .   nne
  suck   dinr
part   or
hey c   n-y
stretch   e b
s one   mc
was c   otc
orison   e b
on doughnuts . . . In Mexico we hc
a word for sushi - bait! . . . I'
asted nicer ointments . . . Pressed ca
has the consistency of chilled

Published in 2007 by
Chicago Review Press, Incorporated
814 North Franklin Street
Chicago, Illinois 60610

ISBN-13: 978-1-55652-651-4
ISBN-10: 1-55652-651-2

Skewered! The Rudest Food Reviews
Compiled by Michelle Lovric

Designed by Michelle Lovric and Lisa Pentreath
Concept, compilation and text
copyright © 2007 Michelle Lovric
www.michellelovric.com
Editorial Assistant: Kristina Blagojevitch
Printed in China by Imago
All rights reserved

10 9 8 7 6 5 4 3 2 1

Readers like mean reviews.
Ruth Reichl

Skewered!

The RUDEST Food Reviews

Compiled by / Michelle Lovric

The proper subject of dinner-table conversation . . .
is savage criticism of the food.

P.J. O'Rourke

CHICAGO
REVIEW
PRESS

Never, ever, point at a photo
in a cookbook and say,
"I'm going to make that."

Julian Barnes

Taste is determined on the tongue
by tiny projections, called villi,
which are able to sense relative
proportions of the four tastes:
salt, sour, yucky and Frosties.

Giles Coren

Because I am both a glutton
and a masochist, my standard
complaint, "That was so bad,"
is always followed by
"And there was so little of it!"

David Sedaris

"The food here was foul until
they killed the chef."

Ludwig Bemelmans quoting a Dutchman
on the cooking on the S.S. *Mesias*
en route to Ecuador

contents . . .

better than **sex** . . . *writing on food*

Food, like sex, is a writer's great opportunity.

Mark Kurlansky

Nobody can be expected to affect academic detachment about something which he puts into his mouth and swallows.

Frank Muir

Food, far more than sex, is the great leveler. . . . Every Napoleon, every Einstein, every Jesus has to eat.

Betty Fussell

The act of eating is very political.

Alice Waters

Hedonistically, gustatory possibilities are much broader than copulatory ones . . . how delightful it is to hear someone describe a magnificent meal, or comical to hear a botched one described.

Joseph Epstein

As a critic, you welcome the rotten restaurant. . . . The accepted vocabulary for accurately describing good food, taste, texture and flavour is pathetically poverty-stricken. When it comes to indicting bad food, however, suddenly the full panoply of language and literature is at your command. No comparison is too far-fetched, no metaphor too odious, no comic turn too outrageous.

Matthew Fort

better than **sex** . . . *writing on food*

Actually, a restaurant critic eats more bad meals than anyone else who cares about good food.

Phyllis C. Richman

It's like *Groundhog Day*. You wake up the next day having eaten a four-star meal, you must go out and eat another four-star meal.

William Grimes

There are two schools of good writing about food: the mock epic and the mystical microcosmic.

Adam Gopnik

I didn't come into the job to make friends, and I've certainly succeeded at that.

Matthew Evans

Occasionally, I get out a black marker and scribble: "I meant it then, but that was before three changes of chef, the new all-you-can-eat policy and that problem they had with the dogmeat in the freezer."

Terry Durack

I was once hung and burned in effigy [at] a bad Chinese restaurant that didn't like the review I wrote.

Alison Cook

restaurant **reviews** . . .

Did they mean to create one of the world's worst restaurants or was it all a tragic accident?

Matthew Norman on Mulberry, London

Bluebird isn't so much a restaurant – more a way of death.

Will Self on Bluebird, London

"Worth a detour" the local guidebook said: I didn't realize that they must have meant it was advisable to go round the village instead of through it.

Keith Waterhouse on a "tarted-up village pub" in north-east England

The food would create an insurrection in a poorhouse.

Mark Twain on the Hôtel de Ville, Milan in *A Tramp Abroad*, 1880

An inferno of blood-curdled oil, Bruegelishly bobbing with tripe and lurking flesh, scabbed with chili . . . looked like nothing so much as the bucket under a field-hospital operating table.

A.A. Gill on the offal stew at Bar Shu, London

The problem is everything you put in your mouth.

Jay Rayner on La Sapinière at Center Parcs Sherwood Forest, Nottinghamshire

restaurant **reviews** . . .

Oh, yuck. Just yuck.

> Grace O'Laochdha on the Egg and I, Minneapolis

I had chosen *côtes d'agneau*. . . . They had been cut from a tired Alpine billy goat and seared in machine oil, and the *haricots verts* with which they were served resembled decomposed whiskers from a theatrical-costume beard.

> A.J. Liebling on a meal at the Prospéria, Paris

I also see from my receipt that I had a dish called "pork dump," which pretty well sums it up.

> Giles Coren on Shanghai Blues, London

The style of cooking is what I think is technically called "fussy old bitch queen, pursed-lip plate fiddles."

> A.A. Gill on Pearl, London

The desserts . . . are served with the same bizarre bowl of schlag (whipped cream). . . . It is designed to improve any dessert, and it would, if only it tasted as if it came from a cow.

> Marian Burros on Ben & Jack's Steak House, New York

Brill, samphire, Jersey royals and sorrel butter served in a parcel sounded so very special . . . served in a double-lined package of greaseproof paper and tinfoil, it had the look of a Christmas present for a cat.

> Giles Coren on Medcalf, London

restaurant **reviews . . .**

The service was like Goldilocks' encounter with the bears.

Todd A. Price on Antoinette, New Orleans

The lobsters – with claws the size of Arnold Schwarzenegger's forearms – are as glazed and tough as most of the customers.

Malcolm S. Forbes on a dish at Palm Restaurant, New York

The WÖK's cooks knew little about cooking, but they were accomplished camouflage experts.

Joseph Wechsberg on a chain of restaurants in Vienna

Like undressing somebody beautiful to find home-made tattoos and bad underwear, the actual eating proved to be a deflating disappointment.

Marina O'Loughlin on Village East, London

"What a madly gay little wine, my dear," M. Cliquot said, repressing, but not soon enough, a grimace of pain.

A.J. Liebling on a thin rosé at Madame B.'s, Paris

Of course, there were a few culinary duds, too, like white asparagus ice cream, peanut-lime-wasabi panna cotta, and duck tongues, which, by the way, taste like duck, but feel like tiny cartilaginous fins in the mouth.

Nancy Grimes on being the dinner companion of her husband, the *New York Times* food critic William Grimes

restaurant **reviews** . . .

They try so hard, go through the most touching preliminaries, give you Gargantuan helpings, rush up trimmings and sauces with the urgency of reinforcements, and the result is something that tastes like the inside of a sofa cushion.

James Agate on a restaurant in Atlantic City
in *The Autobiography of James Agate: a Shorter Ego*, 1946

If only you could eat the design.

William Grimes on the Hudson Cafeteria, New York

My fish soup tasted of no known ingredients. Had I been presented it in a competition I would have settled, uncomfortably, for tomato soup that was a bit off.

Michael Winner on soup at Café Fish, London

Do I detect a fatal tameness, a desire not to offend anyone's uptight mother-in-law?

Gael Greene on Windows on the World, New York

Dining at Chatfield's is like kissing your kid sister – it's just not worth the effort.

W magazine on Chatfield's, New York

restaurant **reviews** . . .

It's the kind of menu that tends to get described as "classic with a twist.". . . In the case of my companion's [meal], a "carpaccio" of raw zucchini dotted with smoked scamorza cheese and diced tomato, the twist was the lack of any kind of flavour.

Tracey MacLeod on Fiore, London

Petits pois . . . came from a can, were small and sort of dented in four places like a sucked-in tennis ball.

Ludwig Bemelmans on the food at L'Oustau de Baumanière, les Baux, France

Food is such an afterthought that, frankly, it's no surprise it's not particularly good.

Time Out on Joe Allen, London

While I wouldn't exactly say my palate was titivated, it was certainly sedated.

Will Self on Blooms, London

I wasn't able to try the "Mousse au chocolat blanc et au Baileys" with – and I'll do this in English – "a deep-fried chocolate tear." When even the confectionery is crying you know it is time to leave.

Jay Rayner on La Sapinière at Center Parcs Sherwood Forest, Nottinghamshire

restaurant **reviews** . . .

Tofu pizza? I could not resist the pizza topped with baby greens, leeks, tofu and fava beans because it sounded like a New Age joke. Unfortunately, it tasted like one, too.

Ruth Reichl on a dish at the Mercer Kitchen, New York

Mall food with fusion pretensions.

Jeremy Iggers on Louis XIII, Minneapolis

This is the worst Japanese food I have eaten all year. . . . Don't you just hate raw fish when it is slightly above room temperature and really, really mushy? When it separates and gaps along the muscle fibers?

Jeffrey Steingarten on Super Sushi, New York

I do not blame the Glade for being what it is – a necessary adjunct of an ignorant and careless world – but it is not for me.

Brian Sewell on the Glade at Sketch, London

Everything about this place is so dreadful that writing about it feels like an intrusion into private grief.

Matthew Norman on the Grill Room at the Café Royal, London

The owners should call a board meeting at once and fire themselves. And, believe me, what I've written so far is kind.

Michael Winner on the Lanesborough Hotel, London

restaurant **ambience . . .**

Ambience is to places what charisma or sex appeal is to people: you either have it or you don't.

Keith Waterhouse

Food is never just something to eat.

Margaret Visser

The modern tendency seems all directed towards spurious finery, meretricious decoration, and uncomfortable New Art.

Frank Schloesser, *The Cult of the Chafing Dish*, 1904

If only some restaurant conceptualists gave the same amount of thought to their restaurants as they do to their lavatories, eating out would be a vastly more entertaining and enjoyable experience.

Matthew Fort

I would, for example, love to have been at the meeting when the marketing boys came up with the name Addendum and then punched the air. To me it sounds vaguely gynaecological, as in, "I'm now going to examine your addendum."

Jay Rayner on Addendum, London

Olica may be the worst name ever invented for a restaurant. It sounds like a fat substitute, or a Macedonian compact car.

William Grimes on the New York restaurant

restaurant **ambience** . . .

I spotted a very striking water feature near the entrance of Hakkasan, in the form of a man relieving himself over some bin bags, while chatting on a mobile phone.

Tracey MacLeod on Hakkasan,
a trendy oriental restaurant in Soho, London

The looming flower arrangements . . . belong around a horse's neck at Belmont Park.

Amanda Hesser on Compass, New York

The beautiful flowers are formally arranged. I would guess the inspiration was "wedding." But the end result is more "funeral."

Richard Johnson on the Rising Sun, Derbyshire

Every penny spent has made it uglier.

A.A. Gill on Bar Shu, London

The place may possibly be even a little too folksy, especially if you do not like cats.

Waverley Root on Chez Anna, Paris

[The wall lights] look like bequests from a Sarasota retirement center.

Frank Bruni on Ureña, New York

restaurant **ambience . . .**

The room is meant to conjure up the glittering halls of the Peterhof Palace and the magic world of Afanasyev's fairy tales. It feels more like a pinball machine.

William Grimes on the Russian Tea Room, New York

I never eat in a restaurant that's over a hundred feet off the ground and won't stand still.

Calvin Trillin

I looked for waiting staff, but the room is so big they were probably obscured by the curvature of the earth.

Jay Rayner on the Corinthian, Glasgow

Grand isn't the word. Cross the threshold and you're in a high-ceilinged phantasmagoria of opulence and clashing styles: classical arches, chinoiserie, huge scallop lampshades, Moroccan-patterned windows and a vast Warholian mosaic.

Time Out on the Belvedere, London

It is so vast that the chef has to use a motorboat to put the noodles in the soup.

Ludwig Bemelmans on the "Cocofinger Palace, Switzerland"
(a parody of the huge Ritz-Carlton, New York)

restaurant **ambience** . . .

It is such a tight squeeze to get into the ground floor room
. . . that one is reminded of the Ollendorf exercises for the
would-be French scholar: "the pocket handkerchief of my
aunt's brother is bigger than the dining room of my sister's
great uncle."

Meg Villars on le Restaurant du Petit Coin, Paris

It reminded me of the 1948 movie *The Snake Pit*, where poor
Olivia de Havilland was trapped in a lunatic asylum.

Michael Winner on Nobu, London

It has, with great panache, expense and devil-take-the-
hindmost braggadocio, transformed itself into the most
laughably hideous dining room in London. No, credit where
credit's due, this is no time to be mealy-mouthed or damn
with faint insult – why should only London bask in its
horrendous radiance? It is the worst dining room in Britain,
including Stow-on-the-Wold, probably in Europe, the globe,
the galaxy, history, eternity, ever.

A.A. Gill on the Dorchester Grill Room, London

Victorian flocked wallpaper runs right up against a retro
seventies pattern that looks like an unfurled spotted ribbon.
Oversize black-leather booths clash with handsome dividers
in polished blond wood. . . . Was there a distress sale at a
catering hall?

William Grimes on Nice Matin, New York

restaurant **ambience . . .**

The gents' toilets combine blood-spattered, stainless steel walls with Kiehl's moisturizer dispensers. Who on earth is Nobu Berkeley supposed to be for? Metrosexual axe-murderers?

Toby Young on Nobu, London

This is one of those "only in Sydney" evenings; a perfectly executed degustation menu presented by its creator – a French master chef and drag queen – served by staff wearing kilts and complemented by a fire-eating illusionist.

Amy Cooper on Slide, Sydney

The chairs appear to have been rescued from the set of *Barbarella*.

Time Out on Ottolenghi, London

One of my fellow critics described Brunello as looking like the inside of Liberace's coffin, but it was more like being in Donatella Versace's underwear drawer.

Toby Young on Brunello, London

A pick-up joint with a sushi bar.

Maria Hunt on Ra Sushi, San Diego

It looks like some kinky duke's S&M chamber. Certainly it's where they hand out the punishment. It starts with the service . . .

Jay Rayner on Ladurée in Harrods, London

restaurant **ambience** . . .

That funky trust funders' hot spot in a Lower East Side back alley where how long you waited for a table depended on which model hung on your arm.

Pasquale Le Draoulec on Freeman's, New York

Do not expect style. . . . This comes under the head of slumming.

Waverley Root on Crêperie Bretonne, Paris

Some of the most pretentious places I've been in have been simple little places in California that scream, "Look how simple I am!"

Jeremiah Tower

The dated red and green décor is redolent of pensioner coach parties.

Time Out on Erebuni, London

Here in full flood, is that style of décor for which the term "Corporate Umbrian" was undoubtedly invented.

Will Self on Garfunkel's in Charing Cross Road, London

When did cushioning go out of fashion and space-age plastics become the material of choice for restaurant seating?

Alan Richman

restaurant **ambience . . .**

Why will people, when they dine out in public places, insist on having music? . . . I cannot bring myself to take my soup in polka time, or masticate my whitebait to the *Intermezzo* from "Cavalleria Rusticana."

Frank Schloesser

In my experience the best food is served in silence.

Waverley Root

Playing music during meals tends to stupefy people and is therefore reprehensible.

Karl Friedrich von Rumohr, *The Essence of Cookery*, 1822

The auricular nerves being intimately related with the nerves of the nose and palate, it is not strange that whatever afflicts the hearing is prejudicial to a process which appeals directly to the taste and smell.

John Cordy Jeaffreson, *A Book About The Table*, 1875

With hindsight . . . the presence of the pianist in the hall didn't augur well. . . . And when we thought it couldn't get any worse, the piano man packed up and what should come drifting through the air of the restaurant but Dido. Mustard gas would have been more welcome.

Gareth McLean on Mar Hall, Renfrewshire

restaurant **ambience** . . .

. . . with one of those pianists who makes you want to proclaim a fatwa on musical theatre.

A.A. Gill on the Dorchester Grill Room, London

It's that special something that makes dining in New York City unlike dining in any other place. Some call it energy. Some call it buzz. New Yorkers call it crowding.

Amanda Hesser

Do not attempt conversation. The brutal acoustics at Nice Matin preclude it.

William Grimes on Nice Matin, New York

It's not anything you'd put on yourself, on your own stereo, at home. Unless, perhaps, you had been asked at short notice to host a humanist funeral for the recently departed pet snake of the strange upstairs neighbour whose tricycle has been chained to the tree in the front garden since you moved in, and whose post always smells of patchouli.

Giles Coren on the music on the Beauberry House website, London

The volume level wavers between loud and deafening and, to push the atmosphere closer to pandemonium, a thundering soundtrack can be heard – or sensed – late in the evening. Mesa Grill is not the restaurant for a heart-to-heart talk, but it's ideal for a screaming fight. Who would notice?

William Grimes on Mesa Grill, New York

pretentious **cuisines** . . .

Who has the time to skin the baby rabbit and dip it in the duck's tears?

Dylan Moran

Does it really matter whether camembert is fried, grilled, flambéed, served naked on a bed of organic doves' hearts or even chomped straight from the box?

Phillip Hodson

People are getting really baroque with their perversions.

Alison Cook

I have known a salad enthusiast who coated each leaf of lettuce with oil on a camel's hair brush.

Frank Schloesser

Making dinner look edible is one thing. Making it look like you've got a team of gay goblin interior designers flouncing over every starter is something else.

A.A. Gill

Any day now, I expect the *Los Angeles Times* to report on the coming of a water sommelier. That's when I head for the hills.

William Garry

pretentious **cuisines** . . .

Canapés, like popes, just emerge from behind a screen with a puff of dry ice. They are held aloft like religious artefacts on votive altars with carved vegetables, they might be the foreskins of saints, or the metatarsals of martyred Jesuits.

A.A. Gill

The sage and orange crusted monkfish risotto cake and chive beurre blanc was a little too fancy for its own good, having been constructed in the fashionable Tower of Babel style.

Victor Lewis-Smith on Number One, Edinburgh

They used to have a fish on the menu . . . that was smoked, grilled *and* peppered. . . . They did everything to this fish but pistol-whip it and dress it in Bermuda shorts.

William E. Geist on One Fifth, New York

I particularly remember a plate piled high with spiny black sea-urchins – unadorned and unopened . . . a foodie's equivalent of seeing the Sex Pistols play the 100 Club in 1976.

Alex Renton on the Globe, London

By the time we get to passion-fruit cloud with its drizzle of coconut-and-olive-oil cream and matcha-tea truffles, we're aesthetically drained. Every dish has three sides and a garnish; every garnish has a garnish.

Gael Greene on Gilt, New York

pretentious **cuisines . . .**

Know that if ever the noble art of cookery be wrecked, it will be upon the quicksands of Fashion.

Elizabeth Robins Pennell, *A Guide for the Greedy by a Greedy Woman*, 1923

Gastronomic nincompoops . . . write of gourmets with a sense of taste so refined that they can tell whether a fish was caught under or between the bridges, and distinguish by its superior flavour the thigh on which the partridge leans while asleep.

Angelo Pellegrini, *The Unprejudiced Palate*, 1948

No two people think exactly alike on Sauces. There are so many schools. The Flamboyant, the Renaissance, the Simplicists, the Natural Flavourites, the Neo-Soho, and many others.

Frank Schloesser

If [the menu] is bound in simulated pigskin like a non-aggression treaty between two very minor nations, its pretensions will be pretentious.

Keith Waterhouse

This was the "Ulysses" of menus, simultaneously awe-inspiring and impenetrable. It was out of control.

Frank Bruni on Megu, New York

pretentious **cuisines** . . .

The sorbet flavors seem to strive for eccentricity, but is there anyone on earth who really wants to eat grapefruit-mustard sorbet?

Ruth Reichl on Tabla, New York

Diners who brave the pig trotter can advance to freshwater eel that's painted with a red-wine glaze, balanced on watermelon cubes and sprinkled with crystallized violets. It works. But it was probably a wise decision to tell the waiters at Atlas to stop reciting every ingredient when putting the food in front of customers. The list invited laughter.

William Grimes on Atlas, New York

It's the death of pleasure when your waiter takes 10 minutes to tell you the bloodline of your tomato. I don't care. I'm already having a bad time.

Anthony Bourdain

The sauces on the menu were all either "encircling" or "enrobing." At the very least they were "complimenting." Sauces around these parts do not, evidently, just hang about and twiddle their thumbs.

Richard Johnson on the Rising Sun, Derbyshire

It's not just rich; it's plutocratic, plumped out with chanterelles and perfumed with truffle oil. In South America, it would be kidnapped and held for ransom.

William Grimes on the pumpkin risotto at Vandam, New York

pretentious **cuisines** . . .

Nouvelle cuisine is the greatest French culinary disaster since ergot in the rye bread begat the Devils of Loudun.

Richard Gordon

Nouvelle cuisine, roughly translated, means: I can't believe I paid 96 dollars and I'm still hungry.

Mike Kalin

Food is to eat, not to frame and hang on the wall.

William Denton

The way I feel about it is: Beat me or feed me, but don't tease me. It's toy food; who needs it? Serve it to toy people.

Jeff Smith

[It] would starve Barbie.

Karina Mantavia on a portion of chicken terrine at World Service,
Nottingham

God, I hate gastropubs. What with all the twice-baked goats' cheese soufflés and geranium-scented panna cotta there's nowhere to put your pint down any more.

Nigel Slater on the British fad of sophisticated pub dining

pretentious **cuisines** . . .

For me, fancy food in a traditional old pub is about as inviting as the phrases "hot male-on-male action," or "tonight Billy Joel live!" or "free prostate exam with every drink."

Anthony Bourdain

I quote from my diary the result of ordering an omelette at a Welsh inn of some pretensions in the spring of 1867: "a tough circular plate of uniform thickness in which onions were the predominant ingredient."

Frederick Pollock, *For My Grandson*, 1933

The club sandwich has been pushed aside in favor of the herb-encrusted medallions of baby artichoke hearts, which never leave me thinking, Oh, right, those! I wonder if they're as good as the ones my mom used to make.

David Sedaris

Nobody likes what we refer to as "scary" stuffing, which is the type with fruit in it.

Hope Davis

Personally I object to cooking simple fare and then dubbing it *à la Quelque chose*.

Frank Schloesser

pretentious **cuisines** . . .

As for the *à la* and *au* this and that, they are often ludicrously misused.

A.E. Manning Foster

I find myself getting phobic about anything "on a bed of."

Bill Nighy

I also hate . . . goujons, medallions, timbales, panachés, coulis, noisettes . . .

Robert Crampton

To send a special messenger to Westphalia to choose a ham, to the West Indies for turtle, to New York for canvas-backed ducks, or to Florence for ortolans and beccaficos, seems an act of pure insanity.

Tabitha Tickletooth (Charles Selby), *The Dinner Question*, 1860

Set it down as a general rule, that no one except Russian Princes, ignorant of our customs, or Manchester men with newly acquired riches, and fools, ever order things out of season.

London at Dinner, or Where to Dine, 1858

The amount of truffle oil a chef uses is inversely proportional to his talent.

Matthew Evans

pretentious **cuisines** . . .

Mashed potatoes and the other fashionable comfort foods
. . . let us feel chic and trendy without having to eat tuna
carpaccio and fava beans.

Jeffrey Steingarten

You, the first parents of the human race, who ruined
yourselves for an apple, what would you have done for a
turkey done with truffles?

Jean-Anthelme Brillat-Savarin, *Gastronomy as a Fine Art*, 1825

The pretentious are always on the lookout for new brands,
tastes and oeuvres outrés (literally, "free-range eggs").

Guy Browning

There must, for me at least, be a faint nebular madness,
dignified no matter how deliberate, to a dinner that is exquisite.

M.F.K. Fisher, *An Alphabet for Gourmets*, 1949

I have nothing against Tall Desserts, Wide Desserts, Desserts
with Lots of Pretty Squiggly Lines or even, on occasion,
Desserts That Substitute Low-Fat Yogurt for Whipping Cream.
I mean, I love a good fad as much as the next fellow.

Ken Haedrich

No one should be intimidated by other people's opinions on
what one should eat.

James Beard

ridiculous **and exotic** ingredients . . .

I've always boasted that I'd eat anything that didn't involve
a bet.

A.A. Gill

Novelty! It is the prevailing cry; it is imperiously demanded by
everyone.

Auguste Escoffier, *A Guide to Modern Cookery*, 1907

There is nothing so vile or repugnant to nature, but you may
plead prescription for it, in the customs of some nation or other.

Tobias Smollett, *Travels Through Italy and France*, 1766

A delicacy is not really a true delicacy at all unless it involves
something patently disgusting. At Champor-Champor, they
serve pan-fried duck breast coated in *kopi luak*. *Kopi luak*
are coffee beans that have been excreted from the arse of
an Asian palm civet. . . . It hangs around the fruit trees of
Java eating coffee beans and, every so often, taking a
dump. At which point, the steaming mound is descended
upon by eager Indonesian entrepreneurs with rustic pooper-
scoopers. They pick the beans out of the ordure and send
them off to decadent Western countries.

Rod Liddle on Champor-Champor, London

I won't eat anything that can look me in the eye; I always
think it's memorizing my face so that it can hunt me down in
the afterlife.

David Leite

ridiculous **and exotic** ingredients . . .

I . . . have supped on soup made of ant larvae, quaffed bowls of blood, dined on dogs and chewed through the guts of animals unknown.

Richard Sterling

I have eaten the still-beating heart of a fucking cobra!

Anthony Bourdain on an experience in Saigon

Stuffing your face is relatively virtuous when you compare what the food fetishists get up to. . . . *Teeny woodland animals' hearts blowtorched in front of their families in dolphin's eye sauce.*

Dylan Moran

The rabbit's brain . . . was extracted at the dinner table, when our host whacked the rabbit's tiny cranium with a hammer. Teaspoons were then distributed, and the split skull was passed around like port.

Hermione Eyre on a pretentious dinner party

There aren't many places . . . where you will find goat consommé with Irish moss and wakame tartlet, ackee whitefish in paperbark with lavender-drenched potato, or Japanese golden plum echinacea ice cream with baby bee or giant hornet honey glaze, or that suggests a glass of pudding wine to wash down a chocolate-covered scorpion, worm or cricket. And, yes, that's real scorpions, worms and crickets.

Matthew Fort on Archipelago (formerly Birdcage), London

ridiculous **and exotic** ingredients . . .

Mexican Armadillo (for 4)	$100.00
Beaver & Beaver Tail	$27.00
Muskrat	$62.00

Menu in Sports Afield Club, New York City, 1960s

At last a dish of frogs' breasts was served, which I took for a chicken stew. But as soon as I tasted it I found it impossible to eat another morsel, hungry as I was. Then three others were brought on, boiled, fried and grilled. . . . Alas! They were only frogs again!

Elisabeth Vigée Lebrun on dinner at a monastery near Turin
in *Memoirs of Madame Vigée Lebrun*, 1904

32

When you're given yak-butter tea – or, as our cameraman called it, liquid gorgonzola – take little sips and smile a lot. I found it very, very hard to keep that down.

Michael Palin

Imagine . . . all the briny funk of the ocean concentrated and melded with the finest sweetened cocoa, and you'll arrive at a flavor that if released in America by Hershey could instantly destroy the company's publicly traded value.

Hugh Garvey on anchovy chocolate in Barcelona

I am pleased to think I have eaten bear's paw at last, and can now refuse it without feeling ignorant.

Paul Levy

"Escargot" is French for "fat crawling bag of phlegm."

Dave Barry

ridiculous **and exotic** ingredients . . .

In truth, as any fool knows, seaweed looks and tastes like the pubic hair of a Rhinemaiden.

Will Self

Canned rattlesnake meat . . . has been available in gourmet food shops and is regarded by far-out eaters or profligate spenders largely as a gastronomic curiosity in the same category as chocolate-covered ants.

Calvin W. Schwabe

The flesh of the peccary (after cutting away the fetid orifice on its back) and of the wild or musk hog, both known under the Indian appellation of quanco in Trinidad, is much preferable to that of the domestic swine.

Peter Lund Simmonds, *The Curiosities of Food or the Dainties and Delicacies of Different Nations Obtained from the Animal Kingdom*, 1859

We ate snot apples, disgusting bushman treats that fill your mouth with slimy, vaguely fruity, viscous gob as if a sheep with influenza had sneezed in your mouth.

A.A. Gill on a meal in the Kalahari Desert

Count C—a has promised to send me tomorrow a box of mosquitoes' eggs, of which tortillas are made, which are considered a great delicacy. Considering mosquitoes are small winged *cannibals*, I was rather shocked at the idea.

Madame Calderón de la Barca, *Life in Mexico*, 1943

ridiculous **and exotic** ingredients . . .

The brain of the fallow deer is a noble thing indeed, extremely tasty and healthful and much better than the brain of pigs or calves, not to say better than dolphins' brains, which, in my view, are the very best of all possible brains, considering that one can eat them during Lent and other compulsory fasts.

Francesco Redi, letter to Dr Iacopo del Lago, September 1689

Their flesh is so strong and fishy, that had not the skins served to make caps, rather handsome, and impenetrable to rain, the penguins would have escaped molestation.

Matthew Flinders, *A Voyage to Terra Australis*, 1814

I also mention the recipe for *menjar de gat rostit* – a dish of roasted cat – given by Mestre Robert in his classic 1520-vintage *Libre del coch*. The cat was skinned and cleaned, and its head discarded. (If you eat the brains of a cat, Robert warns, you will go crazy.)

Colman Andrews

I would prefer to not be offered dog or cat. Given a choice between offending a very nice, very proud (and perhaps very poor) host in, say, rural south-east Asia and violating my deeply held concepts of "pets" and "food," I like to think I'd choke down Fido rather than be impolite.

Anthony Bourdain

ridiculous **and exotic** ingredients . . .

Long pork is New Guinea pidgin-speak for human meat, because of the long bones. I've never eaten it, but if I was hungry I would eat you.

Ray Mears

I believe that if ever I had to practise cannibalism, I might manage if there were enough tarragon around.

James Beard

I had a most interesting interview with these ex-cannibals, one old and two middle-aged men, thanks to Masirewa, my interpreter. He first asked them how they liked human flesh, and they all shouted "Venaka, venaka!" (good). Like the natives of New Guinea, they said it was far better than pig; they also declared that the legs, arms and palms of the hands were the greatest delicacies, and that women and children tasted best. The brains and eyes were especially good. They would never eat a man who had died a natural death. They had eaten white man; he was salty and fat, but he was good, though not so good as "Fiji man."

H. Wilfrid Walker on cannibalism in Fiji in *Wanderings Among South Sea Savages and in Borneo and the Philippines*, 1909

In particular, young ladies should decline larks, and especially larks stuffed with oysters.

E.S. Turner

Fortunately, what people don't know, doesn't hurt them.

Pellegrino Artusi on the ingredients for his chicken intestines omelette

monstrous **prices** . . .

Opportunism, the lifeblood of tourism, is at its most naked and feral when feeding people.

Karina Mantavia

In expensive restaurants it is customary to include in the printed bill of fare a number of *recherché* dishes so costly that there is practically no chance that anybody will order them. They give the menu an opulent and exclusive look, and ordinary customers who come in for steaks are grateful that they are permitted to eat them in surroundings apparently frequented by millionaires.

Flann O'Brien

Sharper than the biting adder
Is the adder of the bill.

Adrian Ross

It used to be that your only risk in eating a fancy meal on the East Side of Manhattan was that you might find yourself dropping the money you had planned to use for the eldest's first semester at Princeton.

Calvin Trillin

Tipping the host $10 is a waste of money; you won't get seated more quickly for anything less than $20. (For $20, I'll wait my turn.)

Phil Vettel on getting seated in a "hot" restaurant

monstrous **prices** . . .

The pricing is so predatory as to amount to brigandage.

Matthew Fort on Tuscan Steak, London

Grown men have been seen fleeing after reading the menu posted outside.

William E. Geist on the caviar restaurant Petrossian, New York

This is a casual dinner place for people with so much cash they deserve to be fleeced. Nothing I say about Cipriani will trouble that client base at all – still, I will say it: YOU ARE BEING ROBBED.

Jay Rayner on Cipriani, London

Don't, don't give a dinner at Delmonico's. I did it yesterday and it is a sin to spend so much money on the belly.

William Makepeace Thackeray on Delmonico's, New York

We finished with bought-in cheesecake, watched my credit card smoulder.

Jay Rayner on Blue Kangaroo, London

For that kind of money a lot of chefs I know will come round to your house, cook you dinner and shampoo your carpets into the bargain.

Will Self on Le Manoir aux Quat'Saisons, Great Milton, Oxfordshire

monstrous **prices . . .**

The lobster steamed with tofu and yuan-yang sauce was the worst thing I've ever eaten for 38 quid.

Giles Coren on a dish at Shanghai Blues, London

Someone is gazing through Windows on the poor mugs inside and having a laugh.

Time Out on Windows, London

The disparity between a restaurant's price and food quality rises in direct proportion to the size of the pepper mill.

Bryan Miller

Marie Antoinette should be living in such an age!

Will Self's reaction to the price of a birthday cake in Jane Asher's cake shop, London

To visit a restaurant where everything is just beyond your means is a miserable way of spending an evening.

Edward Bunyard, *The Epicure's Companion*, 1937

[Checks] are scrupulously honest all over Italy. If here and there in some of the smaller places they happen to add the date to the bill, it is an error, committed in perfect good faith.

George Mikes referring to the time of the Italian lira

monstrous **prices** . . .

The urbane creature had just charged me three francs for a tiny ration of haricot beans and eight francs for a partridge, which, at the first glance, I took to be a conceited quail.

George Augustus Sala on a Parisian restaurateur
in *A Journey Due South*, 1885

But really, when you think about it, the notion of potato skins is the most astonishing rip-off. The idea of flogging people a staple as if it were a titbit could only have been arrived at in a decadent society. You can't imagine people in Somalia flocking to Sorghum-U-Like.

Will Self on Garfunkel's in Charing Cross Road, London

And the edamame [salted soy beans]? For $25, you'd think someone could at least feed them to you, like grapes.

Sam Sifton on Megu, New York

Restaurants are not selling bottled water to keep you hydrated. They sell it because it costs them 75 cents and they can charge $9.75.

Alan Richman

It's not about keeping the customer happy, it's about take per head.

Matthew Evans

chefs and their **egos** . . .

And why, every day, do I have to see chefs in the paper?

Steven Berkoff

The cult of personality has turned the tables in the restaurant. The spotlight . . . is focusing again on the chef, who has burst out of the kitchen, shed blubber, grown pecs and attitude, ripped off his clothes, and become the new rock star, right down to having his own groupies.

John Newton

The idea that chefs create dishes in the way that authors create books or composers create music is a common heresy among chefs. They need to be beaten with the irony stick.

A.A. Gill

There's a bumper crop of "market menus." More and more restaurants are seizing on the romance of those two little words to conjure an image of chefs out in the dewy hours with wicker baskets, picking up the sleekest trout here, the sweetest cherries there and dainty bunches of opal basil over there. . . . Exactly what market are they talking about? Dean & Deluca?

Regina Schrambling – Dean & Deluca is an upmarket deli chain

The only thing bigger than the Sydney restaurant scene are Sydney chefs' egos.

Matthew Evans

chefs and their **egos** . . .

The genius of Carême, however, occasionally led him to a state of self-appreciation which is supreme in its bathos.

Frank Schloesser on the great French chef

I don't want my chefs cute and adorable.

Anthony Bourdain on British "Naked Chef" Jamie Oliver

I'm not a smarmy arse. I don't think you should walk into the dining room and grace tables, standing there like some starched stiff erection, gawping at customers and asking how the food was . . .

Gordon Ramsay on schmoozing the diners

His waiting staff are lined up for lunch service when we pass, and Ramsay pounces on one hapless soul and demolishes him with the crispness of a crocodile crunching a Granny Smith.

Catherine Deveney on Gordon Ramsay

Chicago magazine voted him second in a list of the 10 meanest people in the city.

Alex Witchel on Charlie Trotter, of the eponymous Chicago restaurant

We fire customers a lot.

Charlie Trotter

If anyone is aware of the magnificence and importance of Charlie Trotter it's Charlie Trotter.

Anthony Bourdain

chefs and their **egos** . . .

Nearly all truly dreadful restaurants are run by people who've failed at one profession and thought they'd found an easy touch worthy of their talents.

Keith Waterhouse

Restaurants where the famous celebrity chef has taken the night off (or, more likely, is making a few thousand bucks cooking at a corporate event) should post a notice, similar to the ones seen in Broadway theatres: "The role of our highly publicized head chef will be played tonight by sous chef Willie Norkin, who took one semester of home economics at Scarsdale High School and can't cook worth a damn."

Alan Richman

He is the Stanley Kubrick of New York chefs.

William Grimes on the adventurous David Bouley of Danube

There is in Mr Blumenthal's cooking the reverie of a madman, an attractive candour, the twists and turns of a whirling dervish . . .

François Simon on Heston Blumenthal,
chef at the Fat Duck, Bray, Berkshire

If you gave him a human brain he might poach it lightly in a reduction of 1978 Cornas and top it with a mortarboard made of liquorice.

Julian Barnes on Heston Blumenthal

chefs and their **egos** . . .

Fabrice Canelle, formerly of the Brasserie Savoy in San Francisco, has been pressed into service to feed the multitudes, and unfortunately he has sunk to the challenge.

William Grimes on the Russian Tea Room, New York

If Worrall Thompson had been the chef on the *Titanic* it would have sunk long before hitting the iceberg.

Michael Winner on the heaviness of Antony Worrall Thompson's cooking at Downstairs at 190, London

If it is true, as used to be said, that oversalting means the cook is in love, at least one cook at Le Cirque must be head over heels.

Mimi Sheraton on Le Cirque, New York

Mr Trocca dusts his [foie gras] with yuca flour, and it must be said that yuca dusting does not do much to advance the cause of foie gras. The appetizer feels as if it had been rolled in regular dust.

William Grimes on a dish at Vandam, New York

don't try this **at home . . .**

Where is the rascal cook?

> Petruchio in William Shakespeare's *The Taming of the Shrew*, 1623

You need not wonder that diseases are beyond counting: count the cooks!

> Seneca, *Epistulae ad Lucilium,* 1st century BC

It seems that the main preoccupation of those who cook is to stuff, to fill the stomach as one fills a sack, to excite it and poison it with drugs and evil concoctions.

> V.G. Pennino

People say they're a "good cook." But what they mean is that they can create a splendid dish. Being a good cook really means being resourceful. We've lost the ability to go into a kitchen and throw together what's available and turn it into a satisfying meal.

> Ruth Reichl

The modern kitchen is afflicted by indolence, apathy and lassitude.

> Mimi Spencer

Another sad comestive truth is that the best foods are the products of infinite and wearying trouble.

> Rose Macaulay, *Personal Pleasures,* 1935

don't try this **at home . . .**

The French got it right when they christened the kitchen arsenal the *batterie de cuisine*. Hunger, like lust in action, is savage, extreme, rude, cruel. To satisfy it is to do battle.

Betty Fussell

In cooking, as in love, a little help can be invaluable. . . . Stimulants, therefore, are not only useful but desirable. There are many occasions where a lover or a trencherman would be far below his best form if art did not come to the aid of nature.

Alexandre Balthasar Grimod de la Reynière

Recipe: A series of step-by-step instructions for preparing ingredients you forgot to buy in utensils you do not own to make a dish the dog will not eat the rest of.

Henry Beard and Roy McKie

Even today, well-brought-up English girls are taught by their mothers to boil veggies for at least a month and a half, just in case one of the dinner guests turns up without his teeth.

Calvin Trillin

"Food porn" began to take hold around the world: buyers of lavishly photographed, expensively bound cookbooks gaped longingly at pictures of people doing things that they would probably never try at home.

Anthony Bourdain

don't try this **at home . . .**

The relationship between professional and domestic cook has similarities to a sexual encounter. One party is normally more experienced than the other; and either party should have the right, at any moment, to say, "No, I'm not going to do that."

Julian Barnes on using cookbooks

Attempts to emulate restaurant methods in the private kitchen can only lead to frustration and impotent rage.

Alice Thomas Ellis

Real cooks look dolefully at the photograph of Nigella Lawson's shiny happy fairy cakes and then back at their own dribbling efforts, lined up like the remedial class at school.

Mimi Spencer

A woman who is infallible in her apple pies and successful with her sauces deserves an annual trip abroad. But such, like first editions of *The Faerie Queen*, are rare.

George H. Ellwanger, *The Pleasures of the Table*, 1903

I'm like the anti-Martha Stewart in the kitchen. I'm not about cleaning it up; I'm about looking like a gorilla has come through your kitchen and thrown everything everywhere.

Teri Hatcher

The food in our home was distinguished only for its monotony.

Joseph Wechsberg

don't try this **at home . . .**

I loved my mother very much, but she was not a good cook.
. . . In our house Thanksgiving was a time for sorrow.

Rita Rudner

Family dinners are more often than not an ordeal of nervous
indigestion, preceded by hidden resentment and ennui and
accompanied by psychosomatic jitters.

M.F.K. Fisher

I can still recall my mother's recipe for lumpy gravy.

Lorna Sage

The most remarkable thing about my mother is that for 30
years she served the family nothing but leftovers. The original
meal has never been found.

Calvin Trillin

Imagine us all sitting down to dinner; eight round a pot of
stew. It was lentil-stew usually, a heavy brown mash made
apparently of plastic studs.

Laurie Lee

As a child my family's menu consisted of two choices: take
it or leave it.

Buddy Hackett

don't try this **at home** . . . *men's cooking*

I'm an all right cook. It depends on how much I want to sleep with you, really. I've got a few tricks up my sleeve.

Benjamin Zephaniah

A man who is stingy with saffron is capable of seducing his own grandmother.

Norman Douglas

I don't really cook. I make a mean haricots blancs avec sauce des tomates, on toast with judicious use of Marmite.

Bill Nighy

I tried boiling pig's feet once, but I couldn't get the pig to stand still.

Groucho Marx

I cook a lot now. . . . Some of my creations look a bit odd. Like The Thing That Ate Fulham. Or the Thing That Fulham Wouldnae Eat, more like.

Billy Connolly

Wives may get a kick out of all morning over a hot stove; husbands want something you can pour water on and it's a meal.

Basil Boothroyd

Who bothers to cook TV dinners? I suck them frozen.

Woody Allen

The laziest man I ever met put popcorn in his pancakes so they would turn over by themselves.

W.C. Fields

You end up eating bread from the bag . . . dipping it in anything that is runnier than bread.

Dylan Moran

Simple omelettes. . . . Add contents of refrigerator to two eggs and cook until everything stops wiggling.

P.J. O'Rourke

Barbecues are to cooking what Stonehenge is to architecture: a start.

A.A. Gill

A barbecue . . . nuked on one side and wriggling with salmonella on the other.

Jeremy Clarkson

To your dinner guests you say "flambé"; to the insurance agent you say, "short in the house wiring."

P.J. O'Rourke

dinner **parties** . . . *work of the devil*

"A dinner party": what terrible words they are.

Julian Barnes

It is often argued that sex or death is the last taboo, but I would argue that it is the dinner party. You are meant to like the dinner party, in the same way that you are meant to like flowers or music or children or sunsets.

Craig Brown

Dinner parties are the work of the devil, the dark side of honest supper, twisting the feeding of family and friends to malevolence by snobbery, etiquette, envy and pomp.

A.A. Gill

What is your host's purpose in having a party? Surely not for you to enjoy yourself; if that were their sole purpose they'd have simply sent champagne and women over to your place by taxi.

P.J. O'Rourke

A banquet is probably the most fatiguing thing in the world except ditch digging. It is the insanest of all recreations. The inventor of it overlooked no detail that could furnish weariness, distress, harassment, and acute and long-sustained misery of mind and body.

Mark Twain

dinner **parties** . . . *work of the devil*

It's a dinner party if you write the names of people you know perfectly well on little Alzheimer's cards and stick them into slots in gilt farm animals or scallop shells.

A.A. Gill

There is one female failing in respect to dinners, which I cannot help here noticing, and that is, a very inconvenient love of garnish and flowers, either natural or cut in turnips and carrots, and stuck on dishes, so as greatly to impede carving and helping. This is the true barbarian principle of ornament, and is in no way distinguishable from the "untutored Indian's" fondness for feathers and shells.

Thomas Walker, *Aristology, or The Art of Dining*, 1835

Avoid a house where ostentation is the ruling passion, where handsome plate prevails; where the host, as the old story goes, boasts of his fine gildings, until some waggish guest exclaims, "Never mind your gilding, give us a taste of your *carving.*"

London at Dinner, or Where to Dine, 1858

Today, we cook to impress rather than cook to eat.

Mimi Spencer

The absurd pride of feeling it necessary to "astonish the Browns" when a party is given, is a great check to genial hospitality.

Tabitha Tickletooth (Charles Selby)

dinner **parties** . . . *work of the devil*

It has been my ill-fortune to be introduced, at an otherwise harmless suburban dinner, to a catastrophe of cutlets, garnished with tinned vegetables, and to be gravely informed, on an ill-spelt menu, that it was *"Cutelletes d'Agneau à la Jardinnier,"* which would be ludicrous, were it not sad.

Frank Schloesser

Beware of a party of 18 or 20 in a room that would scarcely hold half the number conveniently; where an influenza trap is laid for you, by the room being at Calcutta heat; the windows and doors open, forming a thorough draught: where the cold clammy entrées arrive in a cart, or a cab, from a second-rate pastry-cook: where everything is sure to be cold, except the wine . . . where a page with three tiers of buttons, his paws encased in white cotton gloves, inserts his thumb into the fish sauces, brings you potatoes, with your *pâté* if you are bold enough to attempt a thick wall of doughy pastry, with a homeopathic supply of oysters unbearded within, and who invariably deposits the contents of same greasy dish upon your coat or your neighbour's dress.

London at Dinner, or Where to Dine, 1858

The humour I am in is worse than words can describe. I have had a hideous dinner of some abominable spiced-up indescribable mess, and it has exasperated me against the world at large.

Charlotte Brontë, letter to Ellen Nussey, October 1841

dinner **parties** . . . *work of the devil*

House-warming at Zola's . . . very tasty dinner . . . including some grouse whose scented flesh Daudet compared to an old courtesan's flesh marinaded in a bidet.

Edmond de Goncourt, entry in his journal, April 1878

In the centre was a bad thin soup, poisoned with celery; at the top a dish of threaded skate, bedevilled with carrots and turnips . . . at bottom roast beef, so-so; at side, ill-boiled beetroot, stewed with a greasy sauce, without vinegar; potatoes, veal cutlets, cold and not well-dressed; anchovy toast and tartlets. Second course: two partridges, ill-trussed and worse stuffed; at bottom, an old hare, newly killed and poorly stuffed; at side, celery and some other trash; in short, a very poor performance on the whole.

Alexander Gibson Hunter on dinner at Dr Hunter's, 1805

53

The repast consisted of elk's meat . . . also the flesh of bear, seal, beaver, and wild fowl. There were eight or ten stone boilers or cauldrons full of meats in the middle of the great hut . . . the Indians ate in a very filthy manner. When their hands were covered with fat or grease they would rub them on their own heads or on the hair of their dogs. Before the meat was cooked each guest arose, took a dog, and hopped round the boilers from one end of the great hut to the other. Arriving in front of the chief, the Montagnais Indian feaster would throw his dog violently to the ground, exclaiming: "Ho! ho! ho!" after which he returned to his place. At the close of the banquet every one danced, with the skulls of their Iroquois enemies slung over their backs.

Sir Harry Johnston on dining with the Montagnais Indians in *Pioneers in Canada*, 1912

dinner **parties** . . . *work of the devil*

One of the ordinary acts of hospitality and civility on the part of the Esquimaux ladies, is to take a bird, or piece of seal-flesh, chew it up very nicely, and hand it to the visitor, who is expected to be overcome with gratitude, and finish the operation of chewing and digesting the delicate morsel.

Peter Lund Simmonds

It isn't so much what's on the table that matters, as what's on the chairs.

William S. Gilbert

A large dinner party where a heterogeneous assortment of men and women are invited just to repay hospitality or because they must be "worked off" is deadly.

A.E. Manning Foster

A duet is delightful, a trio tactful, and a quartet quieting. I cannot advise going beyond that number.

Frank Schloesser

The conversational competition of 12 persons too often begets the clamorous contention that . . . is more prejudicial than any other disturbing influence to gastronomic enjoyment.

John Cordy Jeaffreson

A crust eaten in peace is better than a banquet partaken in anxiety.

Aesop

dinner **parties** . . . *work of the devil*

Dining out is a vice, a dissipation of spirit punished by remorse. We eat, drink and talk a little too much, abuse all our friends, belch out our literary preferences and are egged on by accomplices in the audience to acts of mental exhibitionism.

Cyril Connolly

I don't mind talking to people, but have never overcome the sensation of despondency that descends when I'm confronted by some smug *hors d'oeuvre* and an array of cutlery that indicates the imminence of many courses and hours of claustrophobic detention at the table; the glitter of spittle by candlelight as your neighbour utters a witticism before swallowing a mouthful of meat.

Alice Thomas Ellis

A punster or anecdote monger who retails his worn out wares, without giving his audience time to laugh or even to get a word in edgeways, ought especially to be shunned. . . . The professional punster is a bore, and the retailer of conundrums a still greater one. The punsters, like the Thugs of India, go on a system; they lead their victims up to a certain number of ready-cut-and-dried plants.

London at Dinner, or Where to Dine, 1858

It is particularly important that intentional insults be totally avoided during mealtimes.

Karl Friedrich von Rumohr

flesh and **fowl** . . .

Meat eaters are generally crueller and more ferocious than other men.

Jean-Jacques Rousseau, *Emile*, 1762

A man of my spiritual intensity does not eat corpses.

George Bernard Shaw

I rather wonder both by what accident and in what state of soul or mind the first man who did so, touched mouth to gore and brought his lips to the flesh of a dead creature, he who set forth tables of dead, stale bodies, and ventured to call food and nourishment the parts that had a little before bellowed and cried, moved and lived. How could his eyes endure the slaughter when throats were slit and hides flayed and limbs torn from limb?

Plutarch, *Moralia*, 1st century AD

It is only by softening and disguising dead flesh by culinary preparation that it is rendered susceptible of mastication or digestion.

Percy Bysshe Shelley, *Queen Mab*, 1813

If the hecatomb of animals we have each consumed in the years we have lived, were marshalled in array before us, we should stand aghast.

Peter Lund Simmonds

flesh and **fowl** . . .

Beef generates gross, turbid, and melancholy blood. . . . So if those who partake of it be of a melancholy constitution, they will be subject to the spleen, they will suffer from the quartan ague, they will contract dropsy, and sometimes there will be generated in them eczema, elephantiasis, leprosy, cancer, tetter . . .

Isaac, *On Diets*, 10th century

You know what foie gras is? It's disgusting, it's a sick liver – worse than cirrhosis multiplied by 10.

Brigitte Bardot

Sausages always have had a suggestion of low life – and its undeniable attraction.

Lorna Bunyard, *The Epicure's Companion,* 1937

Have no faith in those bilious monstrosities denominated sausage rolls.

E.L. Blanchard, *Diners and Dinners*, 1860

The same mindset that would add 4-methylacetophenone and solvent to your milkshake would also feed pigs to cows.

Eric Schlosser

Veal is a very young beef and, like a very young girlfriend, it's cute but boring and expensive.

P.J. O'Rourke

flesh and **fowl** . . .

I did not say that this meat was tough. I just said I didn't see the horse that usually stands outside.

W.C. Fields

This is not meat. This is something they scraped out of the airfilter from the engines of the Exxon Valdez.

James Lileks on a recipe in Better Homes & Gardens
Meat Cook Book

"Duck à l'orange" . . . I refuse to eat not only for aesthetic reasons, but on moral grounds, too . . . ducks and humans are the two species with the greatest propensity to commit rape.

Victor Lewis-Smith on the Morangie House Hotel, Tain, Ross-shire

It was . . . a Kurdish insurgent duck that had been interrogated to death by Turkish policemen using rubber hoses, then left in a warm, damp cupboard to emulsify.

A.A. Gill on the duck pâté at the Langley, London

Tougher than a 10-year stretch in the gulag.

William Grimes on duck tabaka at the
Russian Tea Room, New York

I would just as soon eat a cup of warm pus.

Gloria Swanson on chicken served at a dinner party
given by Ray Coté

flesh and **fowl** . . .

Even muscular chickens that do Swedish exercises in the dark are better than turkeys.

'Cassandra' (William Neil Connor)

Even at what the chef considered medium, I am confident that a half-competent vet with a pair of jump leads and a car battery could have had it up and flying again.

Giles Coren on undercooked grouse at Rules, London

A steak is only as good as the cow and the butcher it came from. In this case, the two could have been interchangeable.

A.A. Gill on steak at Le Relais de Venise, London

They arrived so raw you could have drowned swimming in the blood.

Michael Winner on steaks served at Bibendum, London

The name Big Mac is generally supposed to have come about because it is a big McDonald's burger, but in fact it was named after a big raincoat whose taste it so closely resembles.

Jo Brand

I devoured hot-dogs in Baltimore way back in 1886. . . . They contained precisely the same rubber, indigestible pseudo-sausages that millions of Americans now eat, and they leake'd the same flabby, puerile mustard.

H.L. Mencken

flesh and **fowl** . . .

There was roast pork that looked like army food (I'm thinking of the German army, at Stalingrad in the winter of '42, just after they'd eaten the last horse).

Giles Coren on a meal at Throgmorton's, London

The moist, flavorful meat is concealed under a thick slab of crisp fat that would make a cardiologist blanch.

Bryan Miller on Pig Heaven, New York

It was like eating freshly extracted breast implants.

Hermione Eyre on pigs' cheeks

Eat a plate of fine pigs' knuckles
And the headstone cutter chuckles.

Roy Atwell, "Some Little Bug Is Going to Find You," 1915

Boiled mutton is pretty poor stuff to a man with caviar memories.

Groucho Marx

One of the more popular cuts: pressed shank braised with smoker's phlegm. It may take a few tries to get Uncle Hank to hack up enough Lucky sauce, so be patient.

James Lileks on a recipe in *Better Homes & Gardens Meat Cook Book*

flesh and **fowl** . . .

An appalling lamb shank coated in pasilla, ancho and guajillo chilies and then steamed in a parchment bag. It looks like an oversize, stew-filled beggar's purse.

William Grimes on Rosa Mexicano, New York

I had spit-roasted the sucking-deer whole. Lying on its bed of watercress, it reminded me of a domestic cat luxuriating in the sun. I felt quite sick.

The chef in Elizabeth Russell Taylor's *I Is Another*, 1995

Crédit, who had been hunting, brought in the antlers and backbone of a deer which had been killed in the summer. The wolves and birds of prey had picked them clean, but there still remained a quantity of spinal marrow which they had not been able to extract. This, although putrid, was esteemed a valuable prize, and the spine being divided into portions, was distributed equally. After eating the marrow, which was so acrid as to excoriate the lips, we rendered the bones friable by burning, and ate them also.

Sir John Franklin, *Narrative of a Journey to the Shores
of the Polar Sea*, 1823

Rabbits, except in soup stock, ought not to have the honour of appearing at a gentleman's table.

London at Dinner, or Where to Dine, 1858

fruits of the **sea . . .**

As long as I have fat turtle-doves, a fig for your lettuce, my friend, and you may keep your shellfish to yourself. I have no wish to waste my appetite.

Martial, *Epigrams* (bk. XIII, no. 53), 1st century AD

Quite often the worst place to eat fish is beside the sea. People who catch it are not necessarily the best at cooking it, just as gynaecologists are not necessarily the best lovers.

A.A. Gill

Fish gone bad is one bad bellyache.

Richard Sterling

Erythema, urticaria, obscure and painful poisonings, all these await the enthusiastic consumer of shellfish, whether the lobster and *langouste*, the subtle crab, inimitable mussel, elusive crayfish, or delicate prawn and plebeian shrimp.

Lorna Bunyard

I am known to cross a street whenever I see an anchovy coming.

Jeffrey Steingarten

They come from a factory, somewhere in a Dickens novel.

Amanda Hesser on anchovies

fruits of the **sea** . . .

Loup. The fish that is grilled, stuffed with fennel, flambé in brandy and remains quite tasteless.

Evelyn Waugh

The reason that people who detest fish often tolerate sole is that sole doesn't taste very much like fish.

A.J. Liebling

This is the fatal dish that . . . is looked upon by the working man as analogous in its want of toothsomeness with the cold shoulder and sickly hash of washing days.

Tabitha Tickletooth (Charles Selby) on fried sole

This poor fish tasted of despair, of skull-flattening gusts of some clinical malaise. It appeared to have eased itself on to my plate, using a sinister lime sauce as a lubricant, and lay there enjoining me to schizophrenically incorporate its misery. Which I duly did.

Will Self on lemon sole at the Ark, London

"Turbot, sir," said the waiter, placing before me two fishbones, two eyeballs, and a bit of black mackintosh.

Thomas E. Welby, *The Dinner Knell*, 1932

We began with a *truite au bleu* – a live trout simply done to death in hot water, like a Roman emperor in his bath. It was served up doused with enough melted butter to thrombose a regiment.

A.J. Liebling

fruits of the **sea** . . .

We had a miserable trout that made us think of a sickness among the fishes.

Dorothy Wordsworth

The most egregious example is John Dory, stained dark by immersion in red-wine shiso bouillon and surrounded by baby turnips that have been fashioned expertly into tiny corkscrews. The flavors occupy the same space but that's all they have in common. The lack of communication is so complete that it would take a psychotherapist to resolve the situation.

William Grimes on a dish at Atlas, New York

Damn to hell both the recipe and the person who wrote it.

Pellegrino Artusi on frying salt cod in *The Art of Eating Well*, 1891

Nowhere else in the world has anyone thought of burying a shark for a year and then putting it in their mouths . . . tastes precisely like urine, ferocious, vicious, diseased urine. You know the burning sensation of an Extra Strong Mint or a Victory V? Well, imagine that, but with the flavour of a Turkish long-drop lav – in August.

A.A. Gill on an Icelandic speciality

I had a haddock. It was covered with a sort of hard yellow oilskin, as if it had been out in a lifeboat, and its inside gushed salt water when pricked. Sausages and bacon followed this disgusting fish. They, too, had been up all night.

E.M. Forster on a meal served on a British train

fruits of the **sea . . .**

As for my fish, it looked as though it had melanoma. The airless, brick-like batter didn't even cover the fillet . . . and it shattered like theatrical glass when prodded with a knife. Within was something that smelt of the Aswan Dam and resembled the scabrous scrapings from the gut of a long-dead whale.

Victor Lewis-Smith on Harry Ramsden's Express, Glasgow

The otak-otak, a set fish pâté steamed in lime leaves . . . was as close as a man should get to sucking a fishmonger's insole.

Giles Coren on a dish at Awana, London

I've never eaten anything that glows before . . . it turns out to be some kind of salmon sashimi and it may well be the most unpleasant thing I've ever paid for and put in my mouth.

Thomas Sutcliffe on a fish dish at Dans le Noir?, London

[What] looked like a sea mine in miniature was the most disgusting thing I've put in my mouth since I ate earthworms at school. . . . On second thoughts, I preferred the worms.

Matthew Fort on a dish at Opium, Soho

The wacky Godzilla vs. Fried Green Tomato – half a stuffed softshell crab perched with its claws in the air above a fried green tomato – shows Jacques-Imo's at its best.

Todd A. Price on Jacques-Imo's Café, New Orleans

fruits of the **sea . . .**

Bouillabaisse has a lot in common with a Stradivarius violin: everyone has heard of it but no one seems to know what makes it so good.

Joseph Wechsberg

The bouillabaisse, another house specialty, is a crime against nature.

William Grimes on the Oyster Bar and Restaurant, New York

Pressed caviar . . . has the consistency of chilled tar.

William E. Geist

We started with the platter of *fruits de mer*. . . . There is something indelibly 1970s and Roger Moore about these high-rise still lifes of ice and exoskeleton.

A.A. Gill

The *Tutti Frutti de la Mare* . . . has no charm for me. Personally, I would as soon eat a surprise packet of pins.

Nathaniel Newnham-Davis and Algernon Bastard
on fish dishes in Marseilles, France

A salad of spice-rubbed sea scallops . . . was like watching a play with a brilliant supporting cast and a star who phones in the performance.

William Grimes on a meal at Mesa Grill, New York

fruits of the **sea** . . .

Nobody who isn't an otter has ever eaten two whelks at a sitting.

A.A. Gill

Call me a sad purist but I don't think a good prawn should die only to be cut in half, filled with a herb crumb mix and then fried.

Matthew Evans

. . . squid, an animated ink-bag of perverse leanings . . . and whose India rubber flesh might be useful for deluding hunger on desert islands, since, like American gum, you can chew it for months, but never get it down.

Norman Douglas, *Siren Land,* 1911

67

I wasn't so sure about [my companion's] lobster thermidore. If God had intended the lobster to be slathered with cheese, He would have made it a ruminant.

Will Self on Yetman's, Holt, Norfolk

[The lobster] was drizzled with a sickly "barbecue sauce" that tasted as if it came out of a jar and a "dried egg-yolk sauce" that tasted like it came out of a baby.

Giles Coren on a dish at Shanghai Blues, London

It is entirely unwholesome. I never ask for it without reluctance: I never take a second spoonful without a feeling of apprehension on the subject of a possible nightmare.

Lewis Carroll (Charles Dodgson) on lobster sauce

vegetables and **vegetarians** . . .

With the utmost love and respect for all vegetables, without exception, I refuse to accept them as the staff of life.

Frank Schloesser

I really only enjoy food ripped off the carcasses of dumber, weaker species.

Steve Albini

A vegetarian is a person who won't eat anything that can have children.

David Brenner

Vegetarians have wicked, shifty eyes and laugh in a cold, calculating manner. They pinch little children, steal stamps, drink water, favour beards.

J.B. Morton

Hitler was mostly vegetarian.

Michael Hodges

Avoid fruit and nuts. You are what you eat.

Jim Davis

No self-respecting man ever actually wants to eat a vegetable. But like flowers, conversation and clean underpants, they may sometimes be a necessary evil.

John Birmingham

vegetables and **vegetarians** . . .

We kids feared many things in those days – werewolves, dentists, North Koreans, Sunday school – but they all paled in comparison with Brussels sprouts.

Dave Barry

The neighborhood stores are all out of broccoli. Loccoli.

Roy Blount, Jr

Subjectivity doesn't extend to okra. I hope not, anyway.

William Garry

Mushrooms are a flavour, not a food. This is also true of blackberries.

Evelyn Waugh

They are not really good but to be sent back to the dungheap where they are born.

Denis Diderot on mushrooms, *L'Encyclopedie*, 1751–72

The French fried potato has become an inescapable horror in almost every public eating place in the country. . . . They are a furry-textured substance with the taste of plastic wood.

Russell Baker

The potatoes looked as if they had committed suicide in their own steam.

George Meredith

vegetables and **vegetarians** . . .

I'm tormented by caramelized cauliflower. It's suddenly appearing on menus.

Alan Richman

Asparagus with hollandaise should have been an easy opportunity to please, but there was so little sauce that we looked for signs a cat had got there first.

Time Out on a dish at Le Petit Max, London

An aubergine had simply been put in an oven until it was slightly deflated, and then served. It was depressed rather than cooked, and tasted like an aubergine that had just lost its job.

Giles Coren on "tortino di melanzana" at Il Pomodorino, London

Our side order of vegetables, meanwhile, appeared to have been wandering through Death Valley for a couple of days, and were as tasty as they appeared.

Gareth McLean on a meal at Mar Hall, Renfrewshire

The salad bar! This crouched beneath the window, looking for all the world like one of the life-support sarcophagi on the spaceship in the film *2001*.

Will Self on Garfunkel's in Charing Cross Road, London

Fourteenth-century religious paintings first depicted scenes of damnation in which the overweight wandered Hell, condemned to salads and yogurt.

Woody Allen

vegetables and **vegetarians** . . .

We think that the omnipresent bowl of mixed leaves doused in some overanxious acid slime means that there are dozens and dozens of elegant little plants available for our delectation. Actually, it's the same sweaty plastic bag of immigrant, chemically washed, industrially shredded, polytunnel-grown, winegum-coloured slug ration that every supermarket and restaurant uses.

A.A. Gill

What makes the snobbery of the organic movement more insidious is that it equates privilege not only with good taste, but also with good ethics.

Julie Powell

I wonder why no one ever dreams of asking for a second helping of salad?

Keith Waterhouse

A cucumber should be well sliced, and dressed with pepper and vinegar, and then thrown out, as good for nothing.

Samuel Johnson

What is the most disgusting thing you can eat? It's a baby kale leaf. I mean, even cows hate it.

Jeremiah Tower

Side of Slaw ought to be a minor character from *Beowulf*.

A.A. Gill on coleslaw as a side-dish

soups, condiments, **sauces** . . .

No, I don't take soup. You can't build a meal on a lake.

Elsie de Wolfe

The coloured hot water that masquerades too often as soup is unworthy and despicable.

Frank Schloesser

Alas, what crimes have been committed in the name of chowder!

Louis P. De Gouy, *The Soup Book*, 1949

Two inches of burned and clotted cheese over two inches of sodden bread, with a tiny puddle of pallid pink liquid at the bottom.

Jeffrey Steingarten on onion soup at Balzar, Paris

. . . the olive oil used bringing to mind that old quote about Doris Day (I knew her before she was a virgin).

Matthew Norman on oil used at Pintxo People, Brighton

Much modern depravity, for instance, I attribute to the unholy cult of Mayonnaise . . .

Frank Schloesser

Ketchup . . . tastes like a vile concoction of black ink and ginger-beer.

E.L. Blanchard

soups, condiments, **sauces** . . .

Above all things never indulge in high Dishes, rich Sauces, or strong Liquors of any kind, which only serve to overcharge the Body with noxious Humours, and impair the Vigour and Vivacity of the Mind.

Abbé d'Ancourt, *The Lady's Preceptor*, 1752

Ask them to hold the sweetened library paste that passes for gravy.

Marian Burros on Bar Carvery, Rockefeller Center, New York

The pepper sauce looked like some sort of hideous, brightly coloured ichor, which the chicken had ejaculated on dying in order to scare off predators.

Will Self on a chicken dish at the Ark, London

I've tasted nicer ointments.

Jay Rayner on the dill sauce at Blue Kangaroo, London

. . . the "secret sauce," a mustard-based crime against humanity (of course they keep it secret – if they published the recipe, Hans Blix would be out of retirement in five minutes).

Matthew Norman on Le Relais de Venise, London

As to the advertised port sauce, it was viciously acidic, leaving one to question which polluted port – Tilbury? Rotterdam? Odessa? – it had been distilled from.

Jay Rayner on Babylon, London

dessert . . .

Sweets are something to be slightly ashamed of, to be scoffed secretly or else scoffed at.

Tim Richardson

Nightmares thrive best on doughnuts.

Frank Morton

Custard: A detestable substance produced by a malevolent conspiracy of the hen, the cow, and the cook.

Ambrose Bierce, *The Devil's Dictionary*, 1906

I have always suspected that my ice cream is in fact made out of frozen glops of pig fat, soya beans and fish oil.

Peter Cook

I hate chocolate. It is gacky and ugly and obvious and dumb and it wreaks palatal havoc on your mouth.

Giles Coren

You could write all Marco knows about waffles on the head of a pin and still have room for the collected works of Jackie Collins.

Michael Winner on Marco Pierre White

I am a lifelong enemy of tapioca.

Robert Morley

dessert . . .

I refuse to eat any sweet off any menu where the choice is headed "Your Just Desserts."

Keith Waterhouse

For some reason, the waiters are quite taken with phyllo-dough purses filled with molten chocolate. They need to get over it.

William Grimes on the Russian Tea Room, New York

The apple strudel was dense and leaden, but for all that rather tasty. It fell down into my stomach accelerating at 32ft per second.

Will Self on Blooms, London

The dessert "antipasto" (or is that "dopopasto"?) knocks sweet-tooths back into rehab.

The *Sydney Morning Herald* on Pazzo, Sydney

The small, dense poached meringue looks like my first attempt at making "oeufs à la neige" at home. Mind you, I threw mine out and started again.

Terry Durack on the Astor Bar & Grill, London

The coffee flan, on my first visit . . . was the worst I have ever eaten in my life. I ordered it a second time, and it had made a giant leap to mediocrity.

William Grimes on Rosa Mexicano, New York

cheese . . .

The poets have been mysteriously silent on the subject of cheese.

G.K. Chesterton

Cheese is all right in its place, but it don't want to be allowed to lay above ground too long after it has departed this life.

George W. Peck, *Peck's Compendium of Fun*, 1886

For hundreds of years Englishmen have been suspicious of French claims that certain grotty-looking things that howl in the night and shrink back when you approach them with a knife are "merely rap" [ripe].

Giles Coren on French cheeses

It's fun ordering a really smelly one on the internet and watching the postman having to hold his nose.

Nick Park as his creation Wallace on cheese

. . . an assortment of desperate dairy products so terminally cancerous that I had a good mind to remove them from the restaurant and smuggle them thence into Holland, where it is legal to humanely terminate the lives of things that have nothing left in their future but pain.

Giles Coren on the cheeseboard at Pearl, London

cheese . . .

Roquefort, from the English point of view, is Stilton without a college education. Certain asperities and excesses, had they been removed, would have brought it among the double firsts; as it is, we can only give it a pass.

Edward Bunyard

Unsurprisingly, it stinks like a rotting cadaver, but then what is cheese if not the corpse of milk?

Victor Lewis-Smith on Cachaille

I had bright-red carpaccio . . . with slivers of a lush pecorino, the cuteness of which lay in its relative immaturity (it was still laughing at fart jokes).

Giles Coren on Sardo Canale, London

It strikes most observers as a particularly unhappy and vicious child.

Paul Levy on the newly invented Lymeswold blue cheese

Those that made me were uncivil
For they made me harder than the devil.
Knives won't cut me; fire won't sweat me;
Dogs bark at me, but can't eat me.

Traditional rhyme on Suffolk cheese

home and **abroad . . .**

The first thing that invariably perplexes a traveller abroad, when planting his foot upon a foreign shore, is that fulfilment of his wishes which he has been so ardently desiderating; he is dubious of his dinner . . . if he has only chosen for his fare a fowl, it is served up to him after the fashion of Hamlet Senior, in a manner strongly suggestive of fowl "strange and unnatural."

E.L. Blanchard

There is here and there an American who will say he can remember rising from a European table d'hôte perfectly satisfied; but we must not overlook the fact that there is also here and there an American who will lie.

Mark Twain

Tourists, of course, cannot spoil historical monuments, but they spoil food, because the hotelkeeper, unless he has strong convictions about his country's gastronomical heirlooms, will renounce everything and try to please a moving clientele by giving them what they are accustomed to. . . . Standardization is a fatal thing which should be resented, and fought.

X. Marcel Boulestin, *Having Crossed the Channel,* 1934

The British school of cookery, in its mediocre form, is monotony exemplified.

Frank Schloesser

Englishwomen, in fact, have no culinary ideas.

C.E.M. Joad

To the average middle-class Englishwoman food is of the nature of sin, and in her system of domestic economy the crime and the punishment are swallowed together.

Lorna Bunyard

We spend so much of our time thinking about sex – in love, music, literature, art, as well as basically doing it. Why don't we think about food in the same way? The two are so similar and yet there's a lack of romantic respect to food in this country.

Rick Stein

I think we did once give a cook an M.B.E., but he must have rescued some animal from drowning to have deserved it.

Derek Cooper

Britain is the only country in the world where the food is more dangerous than the sex.

Jackie Mason

You can't trust people who cook as badly as that.

Jacques Chirac on British food

79

home and **abroad** . . .

The do say that the Devil never goes to Cornwall because they put everything into a pie down there.

Frank Schloesser

The consequences of a holiday in Britain are usually an empty wallet and a nauseous stomach.

Leo McKinistry

Boiled cabbage à l'Anglaise is something compared with which steamed coarse newsprint bought from bankrupt Finnish salvage dealers and heated over oil stoves is an exquisite delicacy. Boiled British cabbage is something lower than ex-Army blankets stolen by dispossessed Goanese doss-housekeepers who used them to cover busted-down hen-houses in the slum district of Karachi . . .

Cassandra (William Neil Connor)

People assume that because you've eaten bull's penis or grasshoppers, they must be the worst things you've ever eaten – but more disgusting were those huge plates of food they give you in America. Totally tasteless.

Michael Palin

America has given the world peanut butter and jelly doughnuts, the 98-per-cent fat-free turkey breast, three-cheese-stuffed pizza crusts, granola fondue, the festive hot-dog soufflé, and really, really bad kawffee.

Terry Durack

home and **abroad . . .**

Just as Americans don't make good gigolos, neither do they make good gourmets.

Ludwig Bemelmans

In America we eat, collectively, with a glum urge for food to fill us. We are ignorant of flavor. We are as a nation taste-blind.

M.F.K. Fisher, *Serve it Forth*, 1937

Americans are the grossest feeders of any civilized nation known.

James Fenimore Cooper, *The American Democrat*, 1838

Nothing in America tastes of anything.

James Agate

Foreigners cannot enjoy our food, I suppose, any more than we can enjoy theirs. It is not strange; for tastes are made, not born. I might glorify my bill of fare until I was tired; but after all, the Scotchman would shake his head and say, "Where's your haggis?" and the Fijian would sigh and say, "Where's your missionary?"

Mark Twain

In the morning at breakfast they deluge their stomach with a quart of hot water, impregnated with tea, or so slightly with coffee that it is more coloured water.

Constantin François de Chasseboeuf, Count of Volney, *View of the Soil and Climate of the United States of America*, 1804

home and **abroad** . . .

In eating, they mix things together with the strangest incongruity imaginable.

Frances Trollope, *Domestic Manners of the Americans*, 1832

In the United States . . . one stuffs oneself with food which disguises its extraordinary uniformity under a skilful camouflage of artificial colouring which makes you think that a rainbow has fallen into your plate.

Jacques Martin

The only difference between Cleveland and the *Titanic* is the *Titanic* had better restaurants.

Barney Nagler

The French are sawed-off sissies who eat snails and slugs and cheese that smells like people's feet.

P.J. O'Rourke

The rarest thing is a French chef who does not kill you with sauces and seasoning.

Ludwig Bemelmans

The French do *not* know how to eat, because so specialized an art is required to make food eatable for them.

Jean-Jacques Rousseau

It is now just as easy to have a disappointing meal in Paris as it is in London.

Nigel Slater

In a fatal moment you make a choice of [*civet de lièvre au vin de Madère*] and attack it with gusto, until looking up by chance you see an old gentleman, seated opposite, watching you with a strange look of pity; you pause, and ask for an explanation; he bows, shrugs his shoulders, and politely replies, "Monsieur has not been long enough in Paris, or he would not venture on *that* dish!" "Why not?" you say, with rising misgivings. "Merely," replies the old gentleman, with a mysterious look of aversion at your plate, "that the *hares cooked in these cheap establishments have in general short ears and are apt to mew.*"

Tabitha Tickletooth (Charles Selby) on innocents in Paris
who choose the hare in Madeira sauce

[The Italians] have by and large been content with traditional cooking; you can probably count the stems of lemongrass in the entire country on the fingers of one hand.

Jeffrey Steingarten

You are offered a dish called *Bistecca di Vitello* which simply means beefsteak made of veal. If you do not fancy the idea of beefsteak made of veal, you may have beefsteak made of pork, or of lamb, or even of beef.

George Mikes

home and **abroad . . .**

Pasta is not beneficial to the Italians. . . . When they eat it they develop that typical ironic and sentimental scepticism which can often cut short their enthusiasm.

F.T. Marinetti, *The Futurist Cookbook*, 1932

Pasta is made of long silent archaeological worms which, like their brothers living in the dungeons of history, weigh down the stomach make it ill render it useless.

Futurist Aeropainter Fillia

84

This dish, surely more bestial than any other, looks to us like a female chimpanzee in a sentimental ladies' drawing room.

Libero Glauco Silvano on macaroni in sauce

The trouble with eating Italian food is that five or six days later you're hungry again.

George Miller

In Spain, attempting to obtain a chicken salad sandwich, you wind up with a dish whose name, when you look it up in your Spanish-English dictionary, turns out to mean: Eel with big abscess.

Dave Barry

home and **abroad** . . .

The people who are most addicted to chilies are not Mexicans, Sri Lankans or Hungarians, but Serbs. Their consumption of insanely psycho pickled chili has nothing to do with food, it's simply part of their rudimentary, sadomasochistic bonding that involves drink, stomach ulcers and recreational pogroms.

A.A. Gill

Last night I dined at a Russian house, a real Russian dinner. First soup made of mutton, and sour kraut; very nasty and horrible to smell. . . . Then rôti of some common sort; then gelinottes of Russian partridge, which feed on the young sprouts of the pine trees, and taste strong of turpentine.

Elizabeth Gaskell

Everything is side-dressed with dumplings or potatoes or soused cabbage, and what with the cream cake aftermath and the beginnings of sausage and liver paste, basic measurements soon start heaving about like a clipper in a cyclone.

William Sansom on German food

Now unharness the remains of a once cow from the plough, insert them in a hydraulic press, and when you shall have acquired a teaspoonful of that pale blue juice which a German superstition regards as milk, modify the malignity of its strength in a bucket of tepid water and ring up the breakfast.

Mark Twain

home and **abroad** . . .

The story about the Indian and the Cantonese confronted by a creature from outer space: the Indian falls to his knees and begins to worship it, while the Chinese searches his memory for a suitable recipe.

Paul Levy

Looking into a bowl of won ton noodle is like peering into the primordial soup.

Will Self

And to finish there was "Double-boiled Snow Frog with Fresh Ginseng," which turned out to be my old friend, frog's ovaries.

Paul Levy on a Chinese banquet

In Mexico we have a word for sushi – bait.

José Simon

Nothing is more boring than sashimi. Not even Italian movies. When I'm eating raw fish in a Japanese restaurant, I practically pass out in mid-bite.

Alan Richman

It was the chitinous lens that made me feel I was ingesting something truly alien.

Alison Cook on eating fish eyes in Thailand

diets and **binges** . . .

A gourmet who thinks of calories is like a tart who looks at her watch.

James Beard

Can anybody who is supperless, dinnerless, breakfastless, be happy?

Priscilla in Elizabeth Von Arnim's *The Princess Priscilla's Fortnight*, 1905

The man who pays no attention to the food he consumes can only be likened to a pig in whose trough the trotters of his own son, a pair of braces, and a box of dominoes are equally welcome.

Charles de Monselet, *La Cuisinière Poetique*, 1859

Those, on the contrary, to whom nature has denied an aptitude for the enjoyments of taste, have long faces, long noses, and long eyes. . . . Women, whom nature has similarly afflicted, are angulous, yawn at dinner, and live upon whist and scandal.

Leonard Francis Simpson, *The Handbook of Dining*, 1859

One theory is that it is a plot by the international airlines who are seeking to breed, like so many battery farmers, a narrow-buttocked species. This way they can cram more emaciated human beings into their wretched aeroplanes.

William Hardcastle on dieting

To me, an airplane is a great place to diet.

Wolfgang Puck

diets and **binges** . . .

Great restaurants are, of course, nothing but mouth-brothels. There is no point in going to them if one intends to keep one's belt buckled.

Frederic Raphael

There are people who strictly deprive themselves of each and every eatable, drinkable and smokable which has in any way acquired a shady reputation. They pay this price for health. And health is all they get for it.

Mark Twain

Food phobics . . . are at least as troubled as people who avoid sex, except that the latter will probably seek psychiatric help.

Jeffrey Steingarten

Organic food encourages disease and pestilence and should naturally be the preserve of a few loony cultists who plant seed under the full moon and worship cats.

Michael Hodges

If you are what you eat, no wonder most healthy eaters have the mentality of vegetables. Whereas look at all the great stylish wits and brains since time immemorial – what an all-round smokin', drinkin', guzzlin' crew they were.

Julie Burchill

Isn't anyone willing to stand up for excess any more? Or at least sit up?

William Garry

waiters and **waitresses** . . .

Just as a horse knows immediately and instinctively when its rider is an idiot, so a head waiter greets my entrance to a restaurant with a knowing aside to his assistants, "Nous avons a right one here."

Harry Secombe

"I'm very sorry, sir, but the worst table in the room is reserved – would you like the second-worst?"

Keith Waterhouse

A smile to most restaurant employees is like a silver cross to a vampire.

Michael Winner

They are vain, arrogant, grovelling, lazy and unfit. They are worse than muskrats.

Antonin Carême on waiters

Ordering can take on the character of negotiations at a used-car lot. It takes character to prevail and get the meal you want.

William Grimes on Baldoria, New York

Remember that "today's special" may in fact be today's "hard-sell" item. They gotta move it or lose it.

Richard Sterling

waiters and **waitresses** . . .

The most curious element, however, is the wearing of tired and baggy white gloves, which they only put on to bring dishes. It doesn't make the waiters look elegant, but as if they are customs officers preparing to give you an intimate examination.

Jay Rayner on the Montagu Arms Hotel, Beaulieu, Hampshire

A real waiter . . . does not go in for badinage – the tell-tale sign of an amateur waiter who has to prove he is cut out for something better than waiting at table.

Keith Waterhouse

90

. . . to be called Brian by some Tinkerbell from the Antipodes smacks of too casual an egalitarianism.

Brian Sewell on an Australian waitress at the Glade at Sketch, London

It's not everywhere that a waiter's response to an order for medium-rare steak would be "coolio."

Time Out on Fifteen, London

I asked the waiter if he could describe the venison entrée. "It's awesome!" he said.

Amanda Hesser on Compass, New York

Waiters must never "who gets the soup?" interrupt.

Alan Richman

waiters and **waitresses . . .**

There does come a point when the service is so appalling that it cannot help but take over as the main talking-point between the besieged lunch companions; in which event they might as well sit back and enjoy it.

Keith Waterhouse

The service is like herpes: absent for long stretches, and then suddenly impossible to get rid of.

Jay Rayner on Cecconi's, London

We signal the captain, taking time out against the wall. He frowns. He groans. His feet hurt. His ulcer rages. He hates his wife. The risotto will take 25 minutes. Lasagne will take even longer.

Gael Greene on the Italian Pavilion, New York

The gap of time between when we finished our entrées and when we were asked about dessert could almost have accommodated a showing of *The Aviator*.

Frank Bruni on Della Rovere, New York

We tried pathetic appeals to the wandering waiters, who told us "they are coming, Sir" in a soothing tone – and we tried stern remonstrance, and they then said "they are coming, Sir" in a more injured tone; and after all such appeals they retired into their dens, and hid themselves behind sideboards and dish-covers, still the chops came not.

Lewis Carroll (Charles Dodgson), "Journal of a Tour in Russia in 1867"

waiters and **waitresses** . . .

I longed for the comparative sophistication of a Basil Fawlty, or a Manuel whose incompetence was at least offset by a certain stoic affability. Instead, there was pimply-faced hopelessness.

Ginny Dougary on the Hilton, Brighton

I knew our hopes for a great meal were dim when our friendly waitress, after several minutes of strenuous effort, finally turned to the table for help in opening the wine.

Craig LaBan on Ted's Montana Grill, Philadelphia

I can recall now a horrible eidolon of a young cub of a boy waiter who officiated in a Westmoreland inn. I shall never forget his atrocious red head, his mottled face (something like the tablets of compressed vegetable soup), his flapping ears, the huge encircling collar that made his head look like an ugly bow-pot, the fixed grin, half-idiotic, half-sardonic, that distorted his gashed mouth . . . he stamped on your corns in handing you the salt; he spilt gravy over your linen; he never came when he was wanted; he knew nothing . . .

George Augustus Sala, *After Breakfast*, 1864

The waitresses looked, and acted, like guards in a reform school.

Joseph Wechsberg on the WÖK chain of restaurants in Vienna

This restaurant is so chic, they have a special phone number for the superchic to use so they don't have to get ear contamination from being listened to on the same phone as the less chic.

Michael Winner on the now defunct Pharmacy, London

waiters and **waitresses** . . .

I called for a reservation, and the woman on the other end immediately said, "I have to put you on hold; somebody important is on the other line."

Dennis Way Wheaton on Bice, Chicago

Mr X had ordered the dinner, and when the wine came on, he picked up a bottle, glanced at the label, and then turned to the grave, the melancholy, the sepulchral head waiter and said it was not the sort of wine he had asked for. The head waiter picked up the bottle, cast his undertaker-eye on it and said:

"It is true; I beg pardon." Then he turned on his subordinate and calmly said, "Bring another label."

Mark Twain

Hotel dining-room staff, for some reason, are particularly inept at finding a cold tap and turning it anti-clockwise.

Keith Waterhouse

"Sparkling, please . . . and why don't you stiff us in the process?"

Matthew Evans

The waiter's typical, faux-friendly delivery is tinged with the slightest challenge that says, "You're not going to be cheap about this now, are you?"

Alex Witchel on asking for tap water

death by **food** . . .

Statistics show that of those who contract the habit of eating, very few survive.

Wallace Irwin

Most men dig their graves with their teeth.

Chinese proverb

My grandmother's last 25 or 30 meals were nothing but Frosted Flakes. That's kind of how I expect to end up.

Jane Smiley

Comic films abound with sequences where the funny man gets a free meal because there is a fly in his soup, as though that is the most terrible catastrophe that can befall him, or the worst crime that can be committed by the restaurateur.

T.A. Layton, *Restaurant Roundabout*, 1944

Half the suicides, murders, heresies, false philosophies and apostasies that have stained the annals of our race have had their origin remotely in a disordered stomach or liver, from the malassimilation of food.

Frederick W. Hackwood, *Good Cheer*, 1911

Some persons always show temper during the time of digestion, and nobody should then propose plans to them, or beg favours. Marshal Augereau was a special instance of this, for during the first hour after dinner he would kill whoever came in his way, friend or enemy.

Jean-Anthelme Brillat-Savarin

death by **food** . . .

In these days of indigestion
It is oftentimes a question
  As to what to eat and what to leave alone;
For each microbe and bacillus
Has a different way to kill us,
  And in time they always claim us for their own . . .

Some little bug is going to find you some day,
Some little bug will creep behind you some day,
  Then he'll send for his bug friends
  And all your earthly trouble ends;
Some little bug is going to find you some day.

Roy Atwell

It would be nice if the Food and Drug Administration stopped issuing warnings about toxic substances and just gave me the names of one or two things still safe to eat.

Robert Fuoss

We may find in the long run that tinned food is a deadlier weapon than the machine-gun.

George Orwell, *The Road to Wigan Pier*, 1937

I confess that nothing frightens me more than the appearance of mushrooms on the table, especially in a small provincial town.

Alexandre Dumas

Doctor, do you think it could have been the sausage?

Last words of French composer Paul Claudel

Many people claim coffee inspires them, but, as everybody knows, coffee only makes boring people even more boring.

Honoré de Balzac,
Treatise on Modern Stimulants, 1834

But what is coffee, but a noxious berry?

Charles Stuart Calverley, "Beer," 1861

Coffee is the drunkard's settle-brain, the fool's pastime.

Thomas Tryon, *The Good House-Wife Made a Doctor*, 1692

At the end of a perfect dinner I have often been served with coffee which is nothing more or less than a supersaturated solution of tannic acid.

A.E. Manning Foster

English coffee tastes like water that has been squeezed out of a wet sleeve.

Fred Allen

Well, in Europe, coffee is an unknown beverage. You can get what the European hotelkeeper thinks is coffee, but it resembles the real thing as hypocrisy resembles holiness.

Mark Twain